Stress, Coping and Social Support in the Age of Anxiety

Foundation for Life Sciences

ANTONY KIDMAN AM, PhD

Self-Help Manuals also by the author:

Tactics For Change

From Thought To Action: A Self Help Manual

Managing Love And Hate

Family Life: Adapting To Change

Feeling Better: A Guide To Mood Management

© 2005 Foundation For Life Sciences
PO Box 156, St Leonards NSW 2065 Australia (02) 9438 3828

National Library of Australia Cataloguing-In-Publication Data

Kidman, Antony D. (Antony David), 1938- .
Stress : coping and social support in the age of anxiety.

Bibliography.

ISBN 0 646 45154 5.

1. Stress management. 2. Stress (Psychology). I. Title.

155.9042

Published by Foundation for Life Sciences,
PO Box 156, St Leonards NSW 2065 Australia

Designed and produced by Ronald Proft,
New Frontier Creative Services Pty Ltd (02) 9876 1050

Contents

About the Author

Antony Kidman AM PhD is a clinical psychologist and directs the Health Psychology Unit of the University of Technology, Sydney. He is an Associate Fellow of the Albert Ellis Institute for Rational Emotive Behaviour Therapy (NY), A Fellow of the International Academy of Cognitive Therapy and a Member of the Clinical College of the Australian Psychological Society. He has been carrying out scientific research and lecturing for more than 30 years and conducting a clinical practice for 25 years. He has 141 publications to his name including eight books. He was awarded an Order of Australia in 2005 for his contributions to clinical psychology.

Dr Kidman is a frequent guest speaker on radio and television and writes for the media on health and behaviour. His self-help books *Tactics for Change, Managing Love and Hate, Family Life: Adapting to Change, Feeling Better: A Guide to Mood Management, From Thought to Action A Self-help Manual* and *Stress, Coping and Social Support in the Age of Anxiety* are a result of his research and interest in health and psychology.

Acknowledgements

I would like to thank Ron and Kristina Proft for their design and editorial contributions to the production of this book and to Karla Whitmore for her word processing and proofreading.

I would like to make special mention of Janelle, my wife and partner, for her empathy and invaluable feedback on my writing.

Preface

Stress is a term that is used frequently in everyday conversation. In this monograph I have discussed the meaning of the term together with a brief history of stress research over the last 80 years.

The current ideas about stressful events (stressors) and our human response emphasises the importance of how we appraise or evaluate what is happening. One individual perceives redundancy as a catastrophe, another as a challenge and a chance for a new beginning. I describe how you can change an anxiety-provoking interpretation of an event to a more appropriate response so that you can deal with the situation more effectively.

The role of social networks and their value in buffering stressful reactions is shown together with a range of effective techniques to manage anxiety. They include cognitive restructuring, relaxation, exercise and graded (real life) practice. Finally, a series of key points on emotional health maintenance are listed.

The book is written in concise, non-technical language suitable for family members and people in the workplace. It provides straightforward coping strategies for stressful life events that beset us all in this age of anxiety and technostress.

Meaning of Stress

Stress, or more correctly the stress response, occurred as part of human evolution. Whenever animals experienced prolonged exposure to cold or heat, intense muscular activity, loss of blood, perceived threats, fear, ecstasy, these events or stimuli produce what we now call stress or the stress response. Walter Cannon, the Harvard physiologist, first coined the term **fight or flight** response to describe the body's physiological arousal to survive a threat (Cannon 1929). Working with animals Cannon observed that the body prepares to fight and defend itself from a threat, or to run and escape the danger. The physiological response of the body was to prepare itself for movement and energy production and included the following reactions:

- increased heart rate to pump oxygenated blood to working muscles;
- increased blood pressure to deliver blood to working muscles;
- increased ventilation to supply working muscles with oxygen for energy production;
- dilation of arteries to the arm and leg muscles;
- increased fatty acid activation as an energy source for prolonged activity, e.g. running;
- increased blood coagulation and decreased clotting time in the event of bleeding;
- increased muscular strength;
- decreased gastric activity and abdominal blood flow to allow blood to go to working muscles;
- increased perspiration to cool body temperature.

General Adaptation Syndrome

Another prominent early researcher was Dr Hans Selye of Canada who reported on his general adaptation syndrome (GAS) or biologic stress syndrome (Selye 1936). This concept was developed by Selye over a period of almost 50 years and he formulated the definition of stress as the common or non-specific response of the body to any demand made upon it. A stressor is whatever produces stress. The general adaptation syndrome, according to Selye, is made up of three stages:

1. **The alarm reaction:** this is the animal's reaction when it is suddenly exposed to stressful events (stressors) to which it is not adapted or used to.

2. **Resistance:** the animal's full adaptation to the stressor and the subsequent improvement or disappearance of symptoms.

3. **Exhaustion:** since the ability to adapt to a stressful situation is limited, exhaustion will inevitably follow if the stressor is sufficiently severe or prolonged (Selye 1976).

Selye introduced the concept of **eustress** meaning a useful state of arousal or stress and stress that is not harmful. We all need a certain level of arousal in order to function effectively but when the stress level goes beyond a certain point and turns into distress then our performance decreases and vulnerability to illness increases as shown in the Yerkes–Dodson curve (see Figure 1).

The stress-related hormones in optimal doses improve physical and mental performance and mental processing skills, like concentration, making you more alert. Beyond that level performance begins to decrease in efficiency. The optimum level varies amongst individuals. Unfortunately in the age of anxiety many of us are operating in the distress area and need to learn ways to reduce our physical arousal to an appropriate level.

Figure 1:

The Yerkes–Dodson Curve

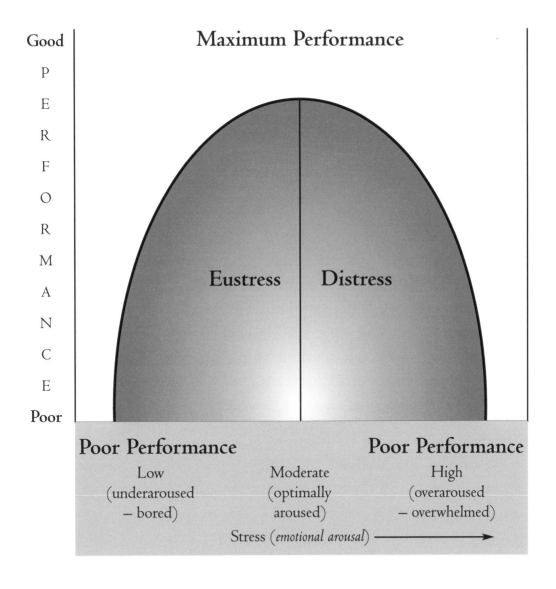

Types of Stressors and Stress Response

Once we have learned our appropriate stress response level we can adapt to the day-to-day stressors of normal living and learn to manage major life crises more effectively. Stressors can be conveniently divided into the following three groups:

1. **Physical:** chemicals, pollutants, noise, temperature, humidity, exercise, health problems, traffic delays.
2. **Social:** life change events such as death of a spouse, marriage, family disputes, workplace hassles.
3. **Psychological:** intense emotions such as frustration, guilt, anxiety, anger, love, hate, sadness, grief, self-downing.

Stressors that produce distress can be divided further into two kinds.

(i) **Acute stress** is the type that appears suddenly, is quite intense and then disappears quickly. An example might be driving along one evening having consumed one or two drinks at a social gathering when suddenly you are pulled over by the breathalyzer for an alcohol test. A feeling of intense anxiety grips you as you wonder whether you might be over the limit. You are probably not but nevertheless for a few minutes once you are flagged down and during the process, you experience all the symptoms of quite intense anxiety. Then once you are told that you are under the limit those symptoms disappear and the stress level immediately recedes.

(ii) **Chronic stress** is the other type that may not appear quite as intense but goes on for extended periods of time. An example might be working for someone whose frequent mood changes and verbal outbursts make your working environment extremely unpredictable and unpleasant. Another example would be living in a city that you really dislike because of the neighbourhood, the weather or the pollution. These chronic stressors are more pernicious than acute ones because your stress response is maintained for long periods and is likely to cause or exacerbate physical illness.

Technostress

How to cope with the rapid pace of technology is the meaning of this term. Weil and Rosen in their book with this title (Weil & Rosen 1998), argue that the revolution in the communication and computer industries will create much additional stress for many people and they will not cope with it particularly well.

Examples of technostressors include:

- **Information overload.** Common examples are the barrage of emails, text messages, faxes and voicemail which continue relentlessly. The reviewing and elimination of unwanted material wastes more and more of people's time.

- **On call.** Individuals' professional and personal lives are becoming blurred with mobile phones, pagers, beepers and palm computers; through these one can be accessed anytime or anywhere. People feel compelled to take these devices to movie theatres, plays, restaurants, and on holidays.

- **Privacy.** The information revolution has eroded privacy in many ways. Every time one makes a purchase with a credit card by mail, phone or the internet, consumer profiles can be prepared with the aid of sophisticated software and your name sold to advertisers to be bombarded with even more blandishments.

- **Computermania.** People now spend more time with chat rooms, internet dating, playing games, surfing the internet, watching computerised television screens and having less live human contact.

- **Planned obsolescence.** Manufacturers of equipment want consumers to throw out VCRs, tapes, even CDs and replace them with a continuing stream of new devices such as iPods, DVDs and a host of interactive systems coming your way.

- **The digital divide.** Many people in lower socioeconomic levels still do not even own a computer. Thus, as the sophistication of computers and the tasks they can undertake increases, people without them will be disadvantaged by the inability to access the information superhighway. The differences between the 'haves' and the 'have nots' will increase further.

Life Events Theory

Two researchers working in the US Navy, Thomas Holmes and Richard Rahe, set out to determine what events in people's lives were most stressful. Thousands of individuals were surveyed and in 1967 they published the social readjustment rating scale (Holmes & Rahe 1967). The scale contained 43 life events, some positive such as holidays, marriage as well as negative events such as divorce, personal injury, illness and retrenchment. All events were assigned numerical values based on their degree of disruption to one's life and the readjustment following the event. They found significant correlation between life event scores and personal health histories. Holmes and Rahe had been influenced by the work of psychiatrist Dr Adolf Meyer of Johns Hopkins Medical School in Baltimore. However, it is important to note that a high score on the social readjustment scale does not predict illness for all people and the model has been criticised. The life events theory does not take into account an individual's appraisal or evaluation of the life experience, e.g. a divorce for one person may be extremely upsetting whereas for another it may be a relief from an unpleasant situation. This has led to stress theories that take into account individual's evaluation of the life events.

HOLMES & RAHE: SOCIAL READJUSTMENT RATING SCALE		
Rank	Life Events	Mean Value
1.	Death of spouse	100
2.	Divorce	73
3.	Marital separation	65
4.	Jail term	63
5.	Death of close family member	63
6.	Personal injury or illness	53
7.	Marriage	50
8.	Fired at work	47
9.	Marital reconciliation	45
10.	Retirement	45

Transactional Models of Stress

The appearance in 1984 of the book *Stress Appraisal and Coping* by Richard Sazarus and Susan Folkman was an influential review of their contribution to the transactional model of stress. Others, including the clinical psychologist Albert Ellis (1962) and psychiatrist Tim Beck (1979), all stress the critical role of interpretation and appraisal of external events and how this affects feelings and behaviour. Figure 2 illustrates this model of stress.

Figure 2:

The Transactional Model of Stress

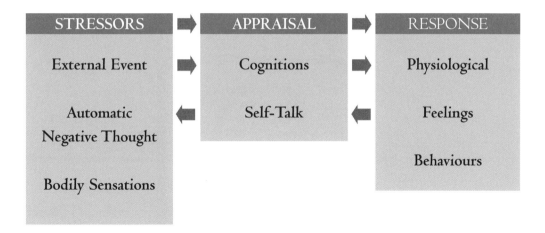

Cognitive Behavioral Model

One of the key strategies in Cognitive Behaviour Therapy (CBT), discussed in more detail later (see Techniques of Managing Anxiety, p. 18), is cognitive restructuring. Briefly, the patient is taught how to reappraise the external world by challenging negative anxiety provoking thoughts about the stressors impacting upon them. (See Figure 3, p. 8.) This changes their stress response to a more appropriate level. A variety of therapeutic coping strategies discussed later are part of this cognitive behavioural treatment.

Figure 3:

The Cognitive Behavioural Model

B. THOUGHTS

You interpret the events with a series of thoughts that continually flow through your mind. This is called 'self-talk'.

C. MOOD

Your feelings are created by your thoughts. All experiences must be processed through your brain and given a conscious meaning before you experience emotional response.

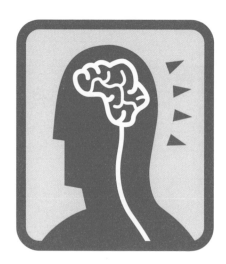

A. ENVIRONMENT

A series of positive, neutral and negative events.

Stress and Health

Stress can affect a person's health (Ogden 2000, Seward 2004) in two ways:
1. by causing changes in behaviour
2. by producing changes in the individual's bodily systems, e.g. the nervous system.

Stress and Behaviour Change

- **Alcohol/drugs/smoking.** Substance abuse is often what people resort to when under stress. This may temporarily relieve anxiety but the downside is the effect on health and the potential for addiction.

- **Self-defeating risk taking.** To reduce anxiety and as a distraction some will engage in gambling, such as playing poker machines, to distract themselves from stressful thoughts. Others engage in risky driving at high speed or tail gating and other aggressive driver behaviour.

- **Exercise avoidance.** People break their normal routines when stressed because they believe they do not have time or energy for normal activities including exercise. This is quite self-defeating as exercise often has an anti-anxiety benefit on the neuromuscular system and a feeling of relaxation afterwards.

- **Overwork.** Many people seem to respond in this way to increasing demands made on them by driving themselves to meet impossible deadlines and workloads rather than delegating or declining to take on more and more.

- **Poor Nutrition.** A common stress response is to overeat or lose appetite. Both responses are unhealthy.

Research suggests that individuals who experience high levels of stress tend to act in ways that increase their chances of becoming ill or injured (Weibe & McCallum 1986).

Stress and Physiological Change

Stress can cause physiological changes in the body (Kidman 1984) as shown in Figure 4.

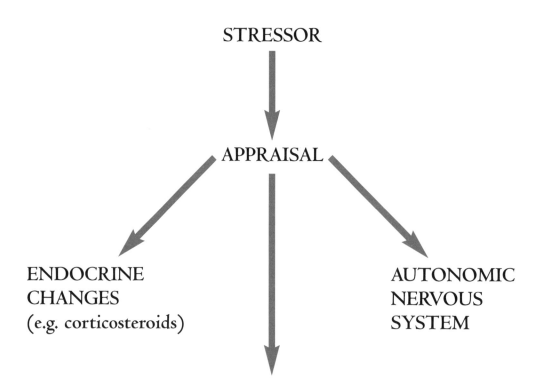

Figure 4:

Stress and Health

STRESSOR

APPRAISAL

ENDOCRINE
CHANGES
(e.g. corticosteroids)

AUTONOMIC
NERVOUS
SYSTEM

IMMUNE SYSTEM
CHANGES

The **autonomic nervous system** produces responses that people know well when they are feeling 'stressed out'. Some of these responses are described earlier in the **fight and flight response** by Walter Cannon. Common, unpleasant, symptoms people report when they experience anxiety as a result of a stressful event include the following:

- numbness or tingling
- feeling hot
- shaky
- fear of losing control

- inability to relax
- abdominal discomfort
- heart pounding or racing
- sweating

The intensity and duration of these nervous system responses vary widely and are terrifying at times.

The **endocrine and immune systems** are affected when people are chronically stressed making them more susceptible to a range of conditions including the following:

- hypertension
- dizzy spells
- rheumatism
- arthritis
- asthma
- tension producing muscular pain
- cramps
- irritable bowel syndrome
- constipation
- diarrhea

- cold sores
- fatigue
- joint pain
- cold
- flu
- ulcer flare up
- clenched jaw
- teeth grinding
- tension headaches
- sleeping problems

Persistent symptoms must be checked by a physician to exclude other pathological causes.

Social Support

The term **social support** refers to the perceived comfort, esteem or help one receives from others. Dr Sheldon Cohen calls it the psychological and material resources provided by others that help one's ability to cope with stress. Social support can be further categorised into different types.

- **Informational support.** This is advice or guidance provided, offered to help people solve problems.

- **Social companionship.** This form of support comes with the participation in group activities.

- **Instrumental support.** This is the provision of physical help and/or resources.

- **Emotional support.** This is the expression of empathy, reassurance and trust, together with an opportunity for emotional expression. It can also include professional help.

Evidence suggests there is a link between social support and health and is the subject of a comprehensive review by Cohen (2004).

Two theories have been developed to explain the role of social support in promoting health.

Stress Buffering

This model argues that assistance from others who provide emotional and material resources help the person cope with stress. An important element in this model is the perception by the stressed individual that others would provide appropriate aid. Cohen found that both student and adult samples reported more symptoms of depression and of physical ailments under stress but these conditions were less among those who perceived that support was available from their social networks.

Main Effect

The **main effect** hypothesis argues that social connectedness is beneficial irrespective of whether one is under stress. People who participate in a social network are subject to social controls and peer pressures that influence healthy behaviours, for example networks might influence whether individuals exercise, drink moderately, eat healthily or take illicit drugs. A wide range of network ties provides multiple sources of information that can promote healthy behaviours. Berkman and Syme (1979) found that healthy adults who are more socially integrated (were married, had close family and friends, belonged to social or religious groups) at the beginning of the study were more likely to be still living at the nine-year follow up than their more isolated counterparts. The association between social integration and mortality has since been replicated in over a dozen respective community based studies (Berkman & Glass 2000).

Social networks also have the potential for negative effects. As well as being subject to the possible negative peer pressure of drugs and alcohol as mentioned above, certain social networks may provide means of contact to spread disease or for participation in criminal gangs. There is possibility of conflict within a group or exploitation such as the membership of a cult.

Personality and Stress

Type-A Behaviour Pattern (TABP) was originally described by Friedman and Rosenman (1974). They described a person with TABP as someone who is engaged in a chronic struggle against time and other people. They include the following behaviours:

- time urgency
- job involvement
- competitiveness
- hostility

Early studies linked TABP with coronary heart disease (CHD); however, subsequent studies have shown contradictory results. A meta-analysis of 83 studies concluded that TABP does appear to be a risk factor for coronary heart disease, approximately doubling the risk (Booth-Kewley & Friedman 1987). The type-A effect has been smaller in studies published more recently than in those done in the early days of the hypothesis.

Anger

Cardiovascular changes with anger are very quick and strong, so it is not surprising that hostility emerges most frequently in CHD research. Initial studies showing a relationship between anger and CHD follows the type-A literature with initially promising results followed by mixed findings (Allan & Scheidt 1996).

A percentage of the population who have Type-A behaviour patterns and a high level of hostility have an increased vulnerability to cardiovascular and coronary heart disease. **Nevertheless, whatever personality we possess we can learn to modify our stress response, especially that of anger, using a variety of techniques.**

Managing
Emotional Responses

Anxiety disorders

- **Generalised or 'free floating' anxiety.** This is characterised by spontaneous negative self-talk that distorts reality. Vague thoughts occur that danger is lurking and such individuals worry about events that occurred in the past or may happen in the future. Worrying about these events will affect you but not the events themselves. It is appropriate to be concerned about things that have happened or may happen and to take appropriate action; it is inappropriate to be so concerned that your ability to function and deal with these events is impaired.

- **Panic disorder.** How many of us at some time have been suddenly overcome with intense apprehension? Such an episode can come out of nowhere but often an initial panic attack can be triggered by a significant personal loss through death, divorce or separation, loss of a job, sickness or financial reversal. Emotionally the individual is overwhelmed with feelings of dread or terror. Physical symptoms occur such as rapid heart beat, muscle tension, perspiration, trembling. The person thinks he may die, go mad or lose control.

- **Phobias.** A phobia is a persistent anxiety reaction that is grossly out of proportion to the stimulus and the reality of the danger. There are a variety of things or activities that produce inordinate and irrational fear in many people – flying, snakes, spiders, mice, water, having to talk with strangers, elevators, crowded places. Even though there is the possibility of, for example, a plane crash or being bitten by a spider the chance of it happening is so low that the emotional response is totally out of proportion to the risk of being harmed.

- **Obsessive compulsive disorder.** Some of us tend to be more neat, tidy and orderly than others. People suffering from obsessive compulsive disorder, however, carry this to the extreme. They spend many hours cleaning, tidying and checking to the point where these activities interfere with normal daily functioning.

Obsessions are recurring ideas, thoughts or images, or impulses that intrude into your mind. Examples include images of violence, doing violence to yourself or others, or fears of leaving things on like lights, the iron, the stove, or leaving doors unlocked. You know these thoughts are senseless and try to put them out of your head but they continue to intrude for hours, days or even longer.

Compulsions are actions that are performed to relieve the anxiety brought up by obsessions. Some people wash their hands numerous times to dispel the fear of being contaminated or they check the locks in their homes over and over again to see that they are secure.

• **Post-traumatic stress disorder.** This can occur in anyone following a severe traumatic experience. These are events that can produce intense fear, terror and feelings of helplessness and include natural disasters like earthquakes, car or plane crashes, assaults or other violent crimes against an individual or their immediate family.

The Anxiety Model

The anxiety model is shown in Figure 5. The external world (A) is perceived and thoughts (B) are generated as a result. Negative thoughts about some future event will then produce feelings of anxiety (C) and unpleasant bodily sensations. This in turn leads to more negative thoughts and increased feelings of anxiety, and thus an ever-worsening cycle is generated.

Figure 5:

The Anxiety Cycle Model

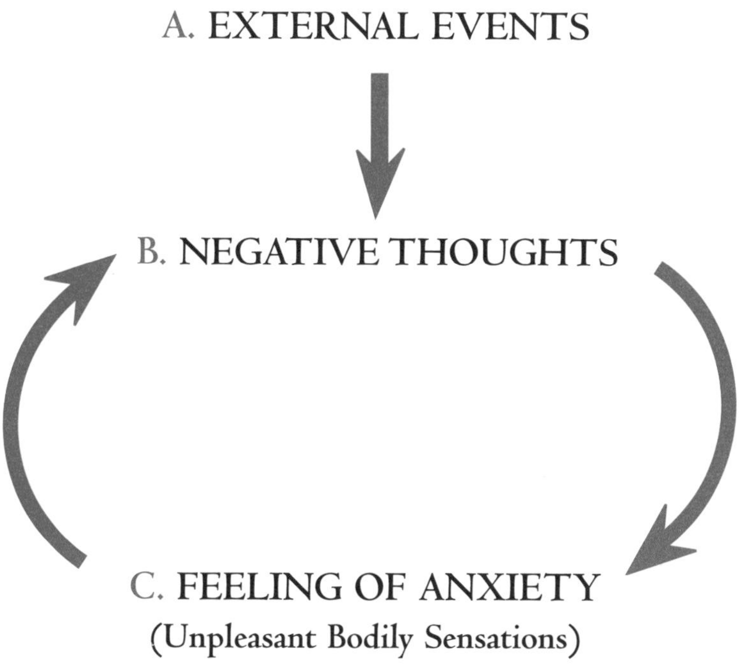

A. EXTERNAL EVENTS

B. NEGATIVE THOUGHTS

C. FEELING OF ANXIETY
(Unpleasant Bodily Sensations)

Techniques for Managing Anxiety

Cognitive restructuring / Rational disputing

Albert Ellis, founder of Rational-Emotive Therapy, was one of the first of the modern cognitive-behavioural psychologists to advocate disputing irrational thinking and to promote this as a tool in psychotherapy that leads to cognitive restructuring. His book *Reason and Emotion in Psychotherapy* (Ellis 1994) lists eleven irrational beliefs which cause disturbance. These include:

1. If there is a chance that something fearful might happen one should keep dwelling on the possibility of it occurring.

2. My life **should** progress easily and smoothly. Things **must** work out the way I want them to. When things go wrong, it's awful and I can't stand it.

Appropriate rational beliefs would be:

1. I had better face up to the reality of the situation, do my best to deal with it and learn to accept that what will be will be.

2. Things are not necessarily going to go as I want and that is unfortunate and I will do my best to overcome obstacles, but if that isn't possible I will accept their existence with the minimum of self-disturbance.

Thoughts that are associated with irrational beliefs produce anxiety and self-disturbing behaviour. For example, you are worrying about the possibility of losing your job due to circumstances beyond your control; the economy is bad and the company is putting people off. The sequence of **thinking ⟶ feelings ⟶ behaviour** needs to be broken and the fundamental technique alluded to earlier is that of **self-talk.**

Self-talk is literally answering your internal critic and disputing the negative thoughts when they enter your head. Let us assume that you may be retrenched because of an economic downturn. Typical negative thoughts may be:

a. 'I am a failure if I lose my job.'

b. 'How am I going to survive if I lose this job?'

c. 'What will my friends think if I am out of work?'

Countering, anxiety-reducing, rational self-talk would be:

a. 'I may fail to hold this job but I myself am not a failure.' 'It is not the worst thing that can happen to me and I can stand it!'

b. 'Thousands of others have survived periods of unemployment and if it is forced on me I will look for another job and try to develop new skills.'

c. 'So what if they think badly of me, I would like them to approve of me but I cannot demand their approval.'

Ellis uses the word **catastrophising** and a great deal of anxiety is generated by the tendency of humans to think of the worst possible outcome when almost always there are other options.

A very useful way to **decatastrophise** is to insert the phrase **'so what if…'** before the thought, 'So what if I get blown up by my boss! I can handle that, I have done so many times before. I will be more cooperative and try to work more effectively, or I will work out a definite plan to get a new job.'

These examples show that writing down negative thoughts and feelings and then disputing them with rational statements can produce a significant reduction of anxiety levels because of rethinking and re-evaluation of the situation.

I believe this is one of the most effective methods of dealing with anxiety, i.e. to recognise the role of automatic negative thoughts and the fact that one generally magnifies the possibility of disaster. You can dispute your thinking and thus break the cycle that intensifies the unpleasant feelings (Kidman 2001).

The following table (Table 1) shows more examples of this method. Table 2 is a disputing form that can be used to practise this method.

Table 1: SELF-TALK EXAMPLES		
Situation	Automatic Thoughts	Rational Response
Describe: 1. Actual event leading to unpleasant emotion, or 2. Stream of thoughts, daydream, or recollection, leading to unpleasant emotion.	1. Write automatic thought(s) that precede emotion(s) 2. Rate belief in automatic thought(s), 1-100%	1. Write rational response to automatic thought(s). 2. Rate belief in rational response, 0-100%
Was thinking of all the things I want to get done over the weekend.	I'll never get all of this done. It's too much for me. 90%	I've done more than this before, and there is no law that says I have to get it done. 70%
Made a mistake ordering supplies.	Pictured my boss yelling at me. 80%	There is no evidence my boss will be angry, and even if he is, I don't have to be upset. 70%
At a function with strangers, felt they were watching me.	People are looking at me. I must be doing something wrong. Perhaps I said some-thing stupid. 90%	I am standing around like anyone else, no one is pointing at me. So people do that from time to time. 75%
Felt my heart start to beat fast as I came into a crowded supermarket.	I am going to have an attack of something and die or go mad. 95%	Nothing is going to happen to me here. People often get strange sensations. I will start breathing slowly. 70%

EXPLANATION: When you experience an unpleasant emotion, note the situation that seemed to stimulate the emotion. (If the emotion occurred while you were thinking, daydreaming, etc., please note this.) Then note the automatic thought associated with the emotion. Record the degree to which you believe this thought: 0%=not at all; 100%= completely.

Table 2: DISPUTING FORM		
Situation	Automatic Thoughts	Rational Response
1. Actual event leading to unpleasant emotion, or 2. Stream of thoughts, daydream or recollection, leading to unpleasant emotion.	1. Write automatic thought(s) that precede emotion(s) 2. Rate belief in automatic thought(s), 1-100%	1. Write rational response to automatic thought(s) 2. Rate belief in rational response, 0-100%

EXPLANATION: When you experience an unpleasant emotion, note the situation that seemed to stimulate the emotion. (If the emotion occurred while you were thinking, daydreaming, etc., please note this.) Then note the automatic thought associated with the emotion. Record the degree to which you believe this thought: 0%=not all; 100%= completely.

Relaxation Techniques

Progressive muscle relaxation

This is a widely used behavioural technique to help manage anxiety. Edmund Jacobsen of the University of Chicago (Jacobsen 1929) introduced progressive muscle relaxation, but the work of Herbert Benson (Benson & Klipper 1977) of the Harvard Medical School and Arnold Lazarus of Rutgers University has been publicised and I would like to draw on some of their findings.

Procedure:

a. Sit quietly in a comfortable position, with legs uncrossed and your feet flat on the floor. Put your hands on your thighs and try to relax.

b. Close your eyes.

c. Tighten and relax certain muscles of your body in a sequence beginning with your feet. When you tense a muscle, notice where it is particularly tense, i.e. scan, then notice how it feels when the muscles are relaxing.

The sequence then is to: (1) tense; (2) scan; (3) relax and (4) enjoy the pleasant feeling.

Next progress to the muscles in your legs, thighs, buttocks, stomach, chest, arms, hands, neck and face.

Now try to relax your whole body and notice any part which is still tense and try to relax it.

d. Become aware of your breathing. As you breathe out say the word 'relax' silently to yourself, e.g. breathe in, breathe out then say 'relax'. Breathe easily and naturally.

e. Imagery. In your mind's eye imagine a pleasant scene, something from the past which was particularly enjoyable or some future event which you are looking forward to. For example, imagine yourself in a beautiful rainforest, you are walking with a friend, the day is sunny and warm, you can hear the sounds of birds and the air is clean and fresh. The sun is coming through the trees and all your worries and concerns have been left behind. There is nothing which concerns you at present ... You could use a beach scene or whatever pleases you ... Remember, imagery is a very important tool in reducing anxiety and it **improves with practice.**

f. Continue this imagery and breathing for 10-20 minutes. You may open your eyes to check the time, but do not use an alarm. When finished, sit quietly for a few minutes, first with your eyes closed, then with your eyes open.

Do not worry about whether you are successful in achieving deep, mental relaxation; maintain a passive attitude and allow relaxation to occur at its own pace. When distracting thoughts occur, let them pass through your mind, and work on your imagery. With practice the response should come with little effort. Try the technique once or twice daily, but not within two hours of any meal as the digestive processes seem to interfere with the relaxation response.

You can practise mini-relaxation sessions at other times, such as when you are sitting in a waiting room, on a bus, or when about to be interviewed for a new job. You can close your eyes, concentrate on your breathing and use imagery even if it's only for 30 seconds or a minute. This will help to calm you and to prepare you for what you are about to do.

I suggest to people who suffer from frequent anxiety to try to relax themselves when they sit. Don't sit on the edge of the chair, don't hunch your shoulders, don't clench your fists. In other words, try to adopt a relaxed posture. Being tense can be very tiring. Allow your body to rest comfortably even when performing tasks; for example, try to relax when eating meals, when waiting in a queue, or driving your car.

Meditation

For thousands of years many thinkers and writers have argued that the mind has always needed respite from thoughts, worries and external stimuli. Meditation is a way to calm the mind from sensory overload. This approach is common to many religions and is characterised by contemplative thought. Zen meditation, one of the oldest forms, comes from eastern philosophy Zen Buddhism (590 BC). Zen meditation is a difficult and disciplined practice, often requiring several hours of motionless, contemplative thought in one sitting. Another type of meditation known as exclusive meditation or concentration meditation involves the restriction of consciousness to focus on a single thought. This single thought becomes a device to wipe out all other thoughts from the conscious state. Practitioners say, 'a single thought is like a gentle wind that blows the clouds away, leaving a clear blue sky'. The presence of the single thought is enhanced by repetition of a word, also known as a mantra, such as 'peace', or one that will exclude other thoughts. Many people in the work-centred lifestyle of industrialised countries have embraced this form of relaxation.

Yoga

The word **yoga** comes from Sanskrit. It means the union of the mind, body and soul. The hatha yoga style places special emphasis on physical postures which are integrated with breathing control. Indian mystics brought the style to the English-speaking world early last century and from the 1970s onward there has been a huge increase in the number of people practising the technique. It is accepted by many mainstream clinicians as a relaxation method and there is no doubt that the stretching exercises improve flexibility; more difficult exercises and postures promote muscle strength and endurance. In general it increases bodily awareness in a society where technological advances have contributed to a more sedentary lifestyle, and further counteracts this by improving posture, muscle tone, flexibility, strength, agility and endurance (Ledell 1983).

Exercise

The techniques already mentioned utilise thinking and imagination to reduce anxiety. I now want to discuss exercise and its role in changing feelings and controlling anxiety.

Any activity which increases heart rate and blood flow throughout the body is classified as aerobic exercise. Good examples of this are jogging, fast walking, swimming, cycling and tennis. All of these can be done readily without going to special classes. Fast walking in particular is one of the easiest and it does not require any special clothing or equipment. Kenneth Cooper, who has written many books on aerobic exercise, recommends that it be performed at least three times a week for a minimum of 40 minutes to achieve and maintain an adequate level of aerobic fitness. According to Cooper, individuals who achieve and maintain this level are able to carry out their daily tasks more effectively, get less fatigued than if they were not fit and enjoy an increased sense of well-being. Before commencing such a program, a medical check-up is essential for a person who has not exercised for some time or is over 30 years of age.

However, in dealing with anxiety we are not so much concerned with aerobic fitness but rather the use of vigorous exercise to help bring about changes in feelings. Thus I tell people that when anxiety starts to mount, vigorous activity can help. The feelings of anxiety will frequently reduce during or at the end of the activity. Imagery can be used during the process and the feeling of well-being that follows a fast walk or workout can be reinforced by a relaxation session using the technique described. I recommend Ken Cooper's book *The Aerobics Program for Total Well-being* (1983) and suggest that an aerobic fitness program could be taken up as a preventive measure for chronic anxiety.

Distraction

Included in this general technique are two methods already described: imagery and physical exercise. They help to replace upsetting thoughts with more appropriate ones. Other activities which can distract and turn off the thoughts that keep bombarding the mind are:

a. Concentrating on what is happening around you. For example, you could listen to someone else's conversation or count how many different blue things you can see. Choose something that engages your attention. When distracting yourself it helps to give yourself a specific task like guessing what jobs people do, or deciding what you would buy in each shop window.

b. Mental activities that include such things as doing mental arithmetic, reciting a poem to yourself, doing a crossword puzzle or pushing yourself to read an article or book.

By utilising one of these activities many people feel better because they have stopped paying attention to their symptoms, which will then often disappear of their own accord.

Systematic Desensitisation / Stress Innoculation

This is a core procedure of behaviour therapy developed by the late Joseph Wolpe (1973).

1. Put yourself into a relaxed state (as described previously on p. 22).

2. Generate in your mind a series of anxiety-provoking situations of increasing intensity.

3. Imagine each scene as intensively as you can with the associated anxiety feelings. Follow each of these scenes with relaxation and coping thoughts as you move up the sequence.

An example of a sequence of situations using this technique could be a woman who is fearful of making contact with strangers. She sits in a chair and imagines the following scenes:

1. People in a crowded bus queue chatting to one another, complaining about waiting. She joins in the general complaints.

2. Relaxation and coping thoughts.

3. She is sitting at a table having lunch when two other people sit down at her table. A conversation about the weather and the quality of the food ensues. She contributes to this conversation.

4. Relaxation and coping thoughts.

5. Sitting in a doctor's waiting room, she initiates a conversation with the person sitting next to her.

6. Relaxation and coping thoughts.

7. She enters a crowded room at a party and starts to chat with some people she does not know.

8. Relaxation and coping thoughts.

9. She phones someone whom she has met only once and suggests that they go out together.

10. Relaxation and coping thoughts.

Many people I have worked with find this a helpful technique.

'In Vivo' Techniques

Another behaviour therapy technique which is considered very effective in overcoming anxiety is to directly confront the person or circumstance as often as you can. This often leads to the realisation that the situation was not so bad after all, and the dire predictions you made about the outcome were misplaced.

A recent case in my experience is that of a client with severe public speaking anxiety. Being a senior executive he was often called upon to speak in public. His anxiety had reached such heights that sometimes he was physically sick before speaking. He was given the behavioural assignment that over the next two weeks he would speak six times at small gatherings within his organisation. He did so and reported that despite feeling extremely anxious at the first meeting, he managed it and by the sixth meeting his anxiety levels were considerably reduced.

A technique described by Albert Ellis to overcome the anxiety about feelings of disapproval from others is to undertake 'shame attacking' behaviour. A typical assignment is to go up to an individual or group of people in the street and simply tell them the time of day. This may seem unusual and prompts a variety of reactions from people, including disapproval and/or puzzled looks. After doing this on several occasions the anxiety about what people will think is lessened. These and other 'shame attacking' assignments enable individuals with a dire need of approval to do things that they have been wanting to do to enjoy their lives more.

Graded Practice

It is best to tackle anxiety provoking situations in a systematic fashion, working up gradually as follows:

1. Make a list of the situations that make you anxious and which you avoid. (See Target List, p. 29.)

2. Arrange these in the order of how difficult it is for you to face them.

3. Select the easiest situation on your list as your first target, plan how to handle it and then start doing it.

4. Make yourself do the thing many times and sooner or later it will become easier.

5. Move to the next item on your list.

Target list

Instructions:

1. Make a list of all those situations that you avoid or which make you anxious.

2. Arrange these in order of difficulty.

3. Express each one in clear terms, and write them in the space provided below.

Target

1. _____

_____

2. _____

_____

3. _____

_____

4. _____

_____

5. _____

_____

6. _____

_____

7. _____

_____

8. _____

_____

Please use another sheet of paper if you need more room.

Planning

I argue very strongly that it is in people's interest to reduce stress in their lives by practising time management. This means preparing a written list of objectives on a daily, weekly, monthly and even yearly basis. In my book *From Thought to Action* (Kidman 2001) I give further details.

By planning one can approach living with a **problem-solving attitude** rather than with an anxiety provoking 'not another crisis' attitude. If you are willing to schedule activities in advance and, most importantly, assign priorities to them, you can decide what short and long-term goals are important to you.

There may be many things you are doing **which you do not really need to do** and only by planning your activities in advance can you decide whether they are important or not. Often urgent demands such as someone insisting that you come and help at a school fete or that you ring back a sales person within the next hour, may not be important for you at all. If so, don't do them.

Systematic preparation of a **To Do Today** list, together with **scheduled periods of leisure or simply doing** nothing, is most important for all of us. Ask yourself, 'What are some of the things I really like doing?' Going to movies, singing around a piano, walking at dusk, riding horses?' Schedule some of these pleasurable activities into your life. (See section on 'Risk Taking' in my book *Feeling Better.*) The rushing around that we see in ourselves and others is not necessary. The 'hurry syndrome' as I call it is often the result of the anxious feelings which occur within us.

The AWARE Strategy

When you suddenly become anxious or panic stricken because of something that has happened, it is difficult to think clearly. It is even more difficult to act appropriately and for this reason, you should learn beforehand what course of action to take.

The key to switching off an anxiety state is to accept it fully; remaining in the present and accepting your anxiety will help it to disappear. Use the five-step AWARE strategy to eliminate anxiety:

1.A Agree to receive your anxiety. Say to yourself 'I'll accept and deal with this!' Your feelings of dread at the thought of it coming upon you again will only worsen by resisting. Instead flow with it. Don't make it responsible for how you think, feel and act.

2.W Watch your anxiety. Think of yourself outside your body as an independent observer watching what is happening. Note how your anxiety level rises and falls. Remember you are not your anxiety. The more you can separate yourself from the experience the more you can watch it.

3.A Act as if the anxiety is not there. Pretend the situation is normal. Act as if you are not anxious. Go with it. Slow down if you have to, breathe slowly and normally, but keep going. If you run from the situation your anxiety will go down for the moment but your thoughts about the situation in the future will bring it back again, perhaps to an even higher level.

4.R Repeat the steps:
   a. Accept your anxiety.
   b. Watch your anxiety.
   c. Act as if the anxiety was not there.

   Flow with the anxiety until it subsides to a comfortable level which it will if you continue to accept, agree, watch and act on it. Just keep repeating these steps.

5.E Expect the best! What you worry about the most rarely happens. Don't be distressed the next time you experience anxiety; instead surprise yourself with your ability to handle it. As long as you live there will be some anxiety in your life. To accept this fact puts you in a better position to cope with anxiety when it next occurs.

As part of the AWARE strategy it is suggested that you monitor each anxiety state by keeping a diary. Jot down a few notes and rate your anxiety on a 0-100 scale. This helps you to separate yourself from your anxiety — to become an independent observer.

Low Frustration Tolerance

Most people dealing with stressful situations and anxiety symptoms feel they **should** not have to put up with these things. This demand, that they lead a pleasant and untroubled life, leads to additional emotional disturbance and the concept of low frustration tolerance.

Most of us start out with a low level of frustration tolerance because of our culture, the media, the way we were indulged by parents and relatives and the general unrealistic expectation that good things should happen to us with the minimum of effort. We **should** obtain high grades in exams, we **should** get a top paying job, we **must** have a fine home and a good relationship, we **must** have a smart car.

When we do not achieve these or any other goals we believe we must have, then we get frustrated, anxious, angry and generally stressed out. The alternative is to replace the **tyranny of the shoulds and the musts** with strong preferences as follows:

'I would strongly prefer to reach these goals but if I cannot achieve some, or even all of them, I will stubbornly refuse to get profoundly distressed. I will be disappointed, but will change my plans and there will still be many challenging and enjoyable things I can strive for.'

Some people are lucky. There is no law in the universe which says there should be justice and fairness to all. Some people inherit wealth, some win a lottery or make a killing on the stockmarket. The majority do not. They work hard for success even then it is not guaranteed; in general **there is no gain without pain.**

In dealing with stressful situations and anxiety symptoms it is crucial to learn how to raise your frustration tolerance level. The first step is to attack the 'I can't stand this...' belief (also known as **'I-Can't-Stand-It-Itis'**). Start telling yourself forcefully and repeatedly 'Yes I can stand it'.

The reality is that you have stood, are currently standing, and could continue to stand, whatever it is for as long as it lasts for as long as you live. This is an objective statement of reality and does not mean that you like the unpleasant situation with which you are coping. However, by forcing yourself to put up with the uncomfortable anxiety symptoms or the difficult people who you have to deal with, you will start to raise your low frustration tolerance. This is the fundamental strategy to increase one's tolerance. It means deliberately seeking out stressful situations from time to time to learn that the discomfort becomes less with repeated practice and that **you can stand it.**

Medication

Drug treatment (pharmacotherapy) for anxiety is frequently used by medical practitioners and is appropriate in certain circumstances (Feldman, et al. 1997). However, there is a tendency to offer anti-anxiety drugs as the main, and for many, the only treatment. The cognitive/behavioural techniques I have described earlier are educational and require understanding by the therapist and the patient. The therapist monitors the treatment and reinforces the patient as treatment progresses.

The drugs that are used to treat anxiety can be divided into four groups and it is important that people know how they act and what to expect from them. The groups are:

1. Minor tranquilisers

2. Barbiturates

3. Beta-Blockers

4. Other compounds

Minor Tranquilisers

Benzodiazepines

Four out of five people taking drugs to relieve anxiety are prescribed minor tranquilisers, which include the range of drugs known as benzodiazepines. These include diazepam (Valium), chlordiazepoxide (Librium), nitrazepam (Mogadon) and alprazolam (Xanax). At higher doses these drugs can be used as hypnotics or sleeping pills; at lower doses they act as anti-anxiety agents. They can reduce acute anxiety when given intravenously.

Undesirable effects: They may make you feel drowsy. They also relax the muscles which may make some people feel a little wobbly in the legs. They may also affect your memory, making you slightly absentminded. They have a good margin for safety and overdose problems are rare. However, large doses of these drugs over a long period can lead to staggering movements, slurred speech and double vision, especially in the elderly. Many people who take benzodiazepines for long periods can become dependent upon them. Studies suggest that after prolonged treatment about 45% of users experience moderate withdrawal symptoms.

Barbiturates

These drugs will both relax you by day and make you sleep at night. They have the longest history in the treatment of anxiety and date back to the beginning of this century. Drugs in this group include amobarbital (Amytal), sodium amobarbital (Sodium Amytal), meprobamate (Equanil; Mepron), sodium secobarbital (Seconal). However, they have been replaced by the much safer benzodiazepines.

Undesirable effects: The use of these drugs has been increasingly restricted because of their toxicity following overdose. They can produce unexpected excitement in the elderly. They also affect the action of the liver. By increasing the rate at which other drugs are utilised by the liver, they may interfere with other treatment the patient may be having. For example, a person may be on a drug to reduce blood clotting, and if barbiturates are taken for anxiety this can change the effectiveness of the bloodclotting drug and cause serious problems.

Beta-Blockers

These drugs have aroused interest recently as they relieve two of the common symptoms of anxiety – palpitations and shakiness. They are mainly used for treating high blood pressure. They are called beta-blockers because of their biochemical action which results in a slower heart rate and thus a lowered blood pressure. If the main symptoms of a person's anxiety are rapid heartbeat and shakiness, beta-blockers may be helpful. One advantage is the low risk of dependency. Drugs such as propranolol (Inderal), metoprolol (Betaloc; Lopresor) are in this group.

Undesirable effects: Because they suppress many of the stimulating effects of adrenalin (a hormone that increases heart and pulse rate, and dilates air passages), Beta-blockers may cause faintness and wheezing particularly in asthma sufferers. Men can experience difficulties with erections because of blood pressure effects.

Other Compounds

Antidepressant medication can be helpful in some anxiety disorders. The selective serotonin reuptake inhibitors (SSRIs) such as fluoxetine (Prozac) and sertraline (Zoloft) are two of the second generation antidepressants. A number of clinical trials have shown these compounds to be effective in the treatment of panic and obsessive-compulsive disorders as have some of the older antidepressant drugs.

Undesirable effects: In general, SSRIs are well tolerated; however, in a small number of patients they cause nausea, diarrhea or transient agitation at the beginning of treatment.

Drug treatment can be appropriate for anxiety, especially to overcome extreme anxiety in some people but for long-term results the person's perceptions and cognitions need to be tackled. Drugs can be helpful to get people into a frame of mind to think about their 'thinking' and to listen to and act on the advice of a professional therapist.

Summary and Reminder

When you are anxious, remember

- YOUR BODILY FEELINGS ARE NOT HARMFUL.

- YOU ARE NOT IN REAL DANGER.

- DO NOT RUN AWAY, IF YOU WAIT, THE FEAR WILL PASS.

- WELCOME THIS AS A CHANCE TO PRACTISE ANXIETY MANAGEMENT. BREATHE SLOWLY. USE THE AWARE STRATEGY.

- CHALLENGE YOUR UPSETTING THOUGHTS AND RECORD THEM IN YOUR DIARY OR USE A SUITABLE FORM.

- DO YOUR RELAXATION EXERCISES.

- DISTRACT YOURSELF.

- USE THIS BOOK.

Emotional Health: Some Guidelines

Emotional health like physical health requires persistence, knowledge and willingness to take responsibility for one's actions and to attack negative thinking.

Characteristics of emotionally and psychologically healthy individuals include the following:

- **Self-direction.** They assume responsibility for their own lives while at the same time cooperating with others. They do not need or demand continuous support from others to survive.

- **Flexibility.** They are flexible in their thinking, open to change and unbigoted in their view of other people. They do not make rigid rules for themselves and others.

- **High frustration tolerance.** They give both themselves and others the right to be wrong. Even when they intensely dislike their own behaviour and that of others, they refrain from condemning themselves or others completely for unacceptable or destructive behaviour. They are willing to put up with difficult circumstances in order to achieve goals, and even though they enjoy pleasurable activities, they are willing to defer them to achieve more satisfying pleasures and happiness in the medium to long term.

- **Acceptance of uncertainty.** They acknowledge and accept that they live in a world of chance, where absolute certainties do not, and probably never will, exist. They enjoy planning and a good degree of order, but do not demand to know exactly what the future will bring or what will happen to them.

- **Absorbing activities.** They are usually vitally absorbed in something. This may include some creative activity or some major human involvement. It does not have to be altruistic but many find that helping others is very rewarding.

- **Enlightened self-interest.** They are interested in themselves and balance their own interests against the interests of others. They are willing to make sacrifices for those for whom they care, but not to become martyrs.

- **Social interest.** Their interest in others is usually sensible and self-helping because most people choose to live and enjoy themselves in a social group or community. If people do not act morally, protect the rights of others and help in the social survival of their society, it is unlikely that they will create the kind of world in which they and their children can live comfortably and happily.

- **Risk-taking.** They are willing to take risks and try to do what they want to do, even when there is a good chance they may fail. They are adventurous, but not foolhardy.

- **Responsibility.** Refusal to blame: they don't blame others for their woes or failures to achieve certain goals. They manager their lives as best they can, practising assertion where necessary and refusing to be walked over. They do not indulge in whingeing and whining.

- **Opinions of others.** They don't allow other people's opinions of them to matter too much. They will listen to criticism from others, even those they don't like, because there may be one or two elements of truth in it.

Facing Reality

THIS IS HOW IT IS

NOT HOW IT
- Was
- Might have been
- Should have been

NOT HOW
- I wanted it to be
- Hoped it would be
- Planned it would be

I ACCEPT THAT THIS IS HOW IT IS

Now I'll get on with my life in a positive way.

Rational Statements

STOP CATASTROPHISING!   THE WORST RARELY HAPPENS

SO WHAT IF……………..?

I WOULD LIKE THE WORLD TO BE A PERFECT PLACE
ALL THE TIME BUT I CANNOT MAKE IT SO,
SOMETIMES I WILL BE TREATED UNFAIRLY.

I DON'T LIKE FRUSTRATION BUT I CAN DAMN WELL STAND IT

THERE IS GENERALLY NO GAIN WITHOUT PAIN

Acceptance Principle

I ACCEPT MYSELF BECAUSE I EXIST,
NO MATTER HOW BADLY I HAVE BEHAVED IN THE PAST
(OR WILL IN THE FUTURE).

I SHALL TRY TO PERFORM WELL
AT ACTIVITIES THAT I CHOOSE TO MAKE IMPORTANT.

I WILL ACCEPT PEOPLE UNCONDITIONALLY
WITH ALL THEIR DEFICIENCIES, BECAUSE THAT IS
WHAT BEING HUMAN MEANS.

IT DOES NOT MEAN THAT I HAVE TO LIKE EVERYONE,
ON THE CONTRARY, I AM PERFECTLY ENTITLED TO
DISLIKE AND DISAPPROVE OF AS MANY PEOPLE AS I CHOOSE,
BUT I WILL NOT CONDEMN THEM AS A WHOLE.

I ACCEPT THAT THEY LIVE, TOGETHER WITH
EVERYONE ELSE ON THE PLANET. I DID NOT PUT THEM
THERE OR ASK TO BE PUT HERE MYSELF;
WE ARE ALL HERE WHETHER WE LIKE IT OR NOT.

IF WE ARE GOING TO SURVIVE AS SOCIAL CREATURES,
WITH A REASONABLE AMOUNT OF ENJOYMENT AND
MINIMAL SELF-DISTURBANCE, WE HAD BETTER PRACTISE
HARD TO ACCEPT OUR FAILINGS AND THOSE OF OTHERS.

WEEKLY PRACTICE RECORD

ACTIVITY	MON	TUE	WED	THUR	FRI	SAT	SUN
Examples: Relaxation, calorie intake, alcohol consumption, exercise, etc.							

Use the above table to record your progress with each activity on a daily/weekly basis.

Bibliography

Allan, R. and Scheidt, S. (Eds) (1996), *Empirical Basis for Cardiac Psychology in Heart and Mind, the Practice of Cardiac Psychology*, American Psychological Association, Washington DC.

Beck, A.T. (1979), *Cognitive Therapy and Emotional Disorders*, International University Press, New York.

Benson, H. and Klipper, M. (1977), *The Relaxation Response*, 3rd ed., Collins, Fount Paperbacks, Glasgow.

Berkman, L.F. and Glass, T. (2000), 'Social Integration, Social Networks, Social Support and Health'. In Berkman, L.F. and Kawachi, I. (Eds), *Social Epidemiology* (pp 137-173), Oxford University Press, New York.

Berkman, L.F. and Syme, L. (1979), 'Social Networks, Host Resistance and Mortality; a Nine-year Follow up Study of Alameda County Residents'. *American Journal of Epidemiology*, 109, 186-203.

Booth-Keewley, S. and Friedman, H.S. (1987), 'Psychological Predictors of Heart Disease: A Quantitative Review', *Psychological Bulletin*, 101, 343-362.

Cannon, W.B. (1929), *Bodily Changes in Pain, Hunger, Fear and Rage: An Account of Recent Researches into the Function of Emotional Excitement*, 2nd ed., Appleton, New York.

Cohen, S. (2004), *American Psychologist*, 8, 676-684.

Cooper, K.H. (1983), *The Aerobics Program for Total Well-being*, Bantam, New York.

Ellis, A. (1962), *Reason and Emotion in Psychotherapy*, Grove Press, New York.

Ellis, A. (1994), *Reason, Emotion in Psychotherapy*, 2nd ed., Birch Lane Press, New York.

Feldman, R.S., Meyer, J.S. and Quenzer, L.F. (1997), *Principles of Neuropsychopharmacology*, Sinauer Associates, Sunderland, Massachusetts.

Friedman, M. and Rosemann, R.H. (1974), *Type A Behaviour and Your Heart*, Knopf, New York.

Holmes, T.H. and Rahe, R. (1976), 'The Social Readjustment Rating Scale', *Journal of Psychosomatic Research*, 11, 213-218.

Jacobsen, E. (1929), *Progressive Relaxation*, University of Chicago Press, Chicago.

Kidman, A.D. (2001), *From Thought to Action: A Self-Help Manual*, 2nd ed., Biochemical and General Services, Sydney.

Kidman, A.D. (1999), *Feeling Better: A Guide to Mood Management*, Biochemical and General Services, Sydney.

Kidman, A.D. (1984), 'Stress, Cognition and the Nervous System'. *Neurochemistry International*, 6, 715-720.

Lazarus, A.A. (1977), *In the Mind's Eye*, Rawson Press, New York.

Lazarus, R.S. and Folkman, S. (1984), *Stress, Appraisal, and Coping*, Springer, New York.

Ledell, L., Rabinovitch, N. and Dalinovitch, G. (1983), *The Sivanda Companion to Yoga*, Simon and Schuster, New York.

Ogden, J. (2000), *Health Psychology*, Ch. 10, 2nd ed., Open University Press, Buckingham.

Selye, H. (1936), 'The Syndrome Produced by Diverse Noxious Agents', *Nature*, 138, 32.

Selye, H. (1976), *Stress in Health and Disease*, Butterworths, London.

Seward, B.L. (2004), *Managing Stress*, 4th ed., Jone & Bartlett, Boston.

Weil, M. and Rosen, L. (1998), *Technostress: Coping with Technology at Work, at Home, at Play*, John Wiley & Sons, New York.

Wiebe, D.J. and McCallum, D.M. (1986), 'Health Practices on Hardiness as Mediators in the Stress-Illness Relationship', *Health Psychology*, 5, 425-438

Wolpe, J. (1973), *The Practice of Behaviour Therapy*, Pergamon Press, Oxford.